Slow Down, Moses

Slow Down, Moses

A Lighthearted Look at People in the Bible

DAVID STEELE

Illustrations by Marshall Potter

Augsburg Minneapolis

SLOW DOWN, MOSES
A Lighthearted Look at People in the Bible

Cover design: Terry Dugan

Cover and inside illustrations: Marshall Potter

Compiled and edited from poems and illustrations first published in *God Must Have a Sense of Humor* copyright © 1983 David Steele (St. Helena, CA: Illuminations Press) and *Dr. Goliath* copyright © 1987 David Steele (Pittsburgh: Hiram Dickens Press).

Library of Congress Cataloging-in-Publication Data

Steele, David, 1931–
Slow down, Moses : a lighthearted look at people from the Bible / David Steele.
p. cm.
Reprint. Originally published: St. Helena, Calif. : Illuminations Press, c1983.
ISBN 0-8066-2464-7 (alk. paper)
1. Bible—History of Biblical events—Poetry. I. Title.
PS3569.T338427S55 1990
811'.54—dc20 90-31263
CIP

The paper used in this publication meets the minimum requirements of American National Standard for Information Sciences—Permanence of Paper for Printed Library Materials, ANSI Z329.48-1984. ∞™

Manufactured in the U.S.A. AF 9-2464

94 93 92 91 90 1 2 3 4 5 6 7 8 9 10

Contents

Preface

Books about God seldom smile. They are serious and solemn and ponderous! This is a book about God. It is designed to smile. We need to catch the twinkle in God's eye.

God must have a sense of humor. God is the Author of life. All that we have and are comes from God. And that includes humor. It is a gift of grace. It is meant to be used at home, at work, and—heaven forbid—in church!

We yearn to be close to God. God loves us and seeks us. Yet we keep God at a distance. How? The Bible and human experience are clear on this. It is our human pride that holds God off. Pride is the ultimate sin.

We manufacture grandiose opinions of ourselves. We pose; we preen; we strut. We pretend that we are God Almighty! And this "Godalmightyness" shuts God out. How sad! How silly!

For we have, right at hand, a rapier that can swiftly puncture our pride balloons. It is humor, God's gift to us—our finest weapon for attacking hypocrisy. We use it to laugh at others, but too infrequently do we laugh at ourselves. How can God touch us until we do?

An old Jewish proverb states: "When you are hungry, sing; when you are hurt, laugh." The rabbis understood the healing quality of humor. In days of persecution and suffering, they often brought solace to the soul in torment with a smile.

Modern medicine is rediscovering the therapeutic value of laughter. We are hearing how humor has been a servant to healing. Humor is God's gift to people in distress.

But how hard it has been for Christians to sense the grace in humor. Too often we have listened to the angel's words: "Behold, I bring you good news of great joy!" in a solemn, tedious manner. Our worship is serious business. Too serious! Blessed is the congregation that has discovered a smile passing from person to person, a chuckle growing into a communal guffaw, and the warmth of the good news invading the sanctuary through humor.

We want to touch God. Or better, we want God to touch us. So we turn to the Bible. It is the source book of faith. But it is so hard, so solemn!

We talk about "serious Bible study." And that's what our study is: terribly serious. Groups of earnest Christians sit on straight-backed chairs; frowns touch their knitted brows; pious words cross their tight lips—that is Bible study. It is seldom much fun.

What if we learned to read the Bible with a sense of humor? Do we dare approach The Word in a lighthearted way? It may be that God's gift of humor could be the key that will help us relax with The Book. We might discover all sorts of things we have missed in our "serious" study. It is worth a try.

The passages that follow have a theme. They are about the minor events and characters in the Bible. Here are people like us. Read each passage of Scripture with your sense of humor showing. Try to picture yourself in the situation and sense how you would feel.

The meditations are my own response to the passage. As you read them allow the chuckles to come and groan at the terrible puns. If some insight strikes, return to the Bible, see it again in the text. Allow some time for God's Spirit to touch you.

The approach we are taking is lighthearted but not lightheaded. It intends to make Bible reading fun but does not make fun of the reading nor make it funny. We are simply taking hold of God's gift of humor to open up the Word. A person sometimes sees more clearly with a twinkle in the eye.

Leo Rosten defines humor as "The affectionate communication of insight." God grant you may find it so.

San Rafael, California — DAVID STEELE

Slow Down, Moses

Exodus 18:1-27

Now I imagine few of us
Would care to lead an exodus.
For who among us really craves
To lead a horde of former slaves
With all their problems, hopes, and fears
A-wandering for forty years?

Directing an emerging nation
Is a prophetable occupation,
And he who takes the job will be
Assured a place in history.
He'll have no little claim to fame;
Most everyone will know his name.
Prestige, at first, will seem quite nice;
But then he'll have to pay the price.

Moses did not want to grip
The lonely role of leadership,
But God, one brilliant desert dawn,
Commanded him to take it on;
And feeling he could ill afford
To disobey the Living Lord,
He acquiesced to God's request
And gave the job his very best.

No enterprise will long survive
Whose leader works from nine to five.
So Moses, being in his prime,
Began to work some overtime.
His office soon became the site
Of meetings nearly every night.
And then he'd take a healthy tome
Of paperwork to do at home.
It wasn't long before he'd scoff
At any thought of taking off.
With so much work that must be done
He hadn't time for play or fun,
Nor could he laugh, relax, or frolic.
Moses was a workaholic.

Now men with hefty power drives
Are seldom heroes to their wives.
The man who leads a busy life
Has little time for home or wife.
Spouses do not have a yen
To join in praising famous men.
They give success a cool reception
And Zipporah was no exception.

The placid Moses whom she married
Was tired, edgy, tense, and harried.
And she suspected he was very
Ready for a coronary.
And so, she felt, 'twas time she had
A little chat with mom and dad.

She journeyed where her parents dwelt
And told her folks just how she felt.
"I didn't want a bed of roses
When I agreed to marry Moses.
I know it takes a lot of gall
To argue with a holy call,
But Moses, as you clearly see,
Has time for God—but not for me.
I cry myself to sleep at night.
Tell me, do you think that's right?"

It caused those parents great distress
To see their child's unhappiness.
And Jethro, dear Zipporah's dad,
Was more than just a trifle mad.
"The time," he thought, "is overdue
To teach that boy a thing or two."

Jethro's temper rankled raw
As he sought his son-in-law.
But then he saw, to his dismay,
How Moses spent the working day.
People came from far and near
In hopes of catching Moses' ear.
No problem was too small to mention;
They brought them all to his attention.
The sheer amount of people who
Were waiting for an interview
Caused Jethro to feel rather dizzy.
"My son-in-law is much too busy!
I think I'll play a bit of cupid.
That boy's not bad—he's simply stupid."

And so, I'm happy to relate,
Jethro told it to him straight:
"Whoever said you were commanded
To run this country single-handed?
You know you're just the protégé
Of God, who rests the seventh day.
Why you've become (that's very odd)
More indispensable than God.
This schedule you are keeping will
Put you to bed in Ulcerville—
And that's a price we can't afford.
So get some help! Thus saith the Lord!"

Under Jethro's gentle nudges
Moses chose some able judges.
(And discovered to his glee
They did the job as well as he.)

There's ample help for any task—
Once we have the sense to ask!

PLAY BALL!

Let the Children Come

Mark 10:13-16

There's nothing so nice as some children.
Every family should have one or two.
They are such a fine race
When they're kept in their place,
Say . . . the nursery, the park, or the zoo.

In his place a young child is delightful,
Full of fun, a most int'resting buddy;
But her yearning for action
Can cause a distraction
When she has invaded the study.

The office is no place for children.
They foul up our work with their fun.
So we make it a rule
That they must go to school
So their elders can get something done.

Some children came searching for Jesus.
His friends were distressed, and inclined
To think 'twould be terrible
To have a fresh parable
Suddenly slip from his mind.

So they tried to get rid of the children—
Surely no major disgrace—
Protecting their master
From some great disaster,
By keeping the children in place.

"Let those children in," Jesus shouted,
And said something frightfully odd.
"They are bearers of grace,
And their ultimate place
Is right smack in the kingdom of God."

So the place of a child is the kingdom!
That's what he so carefully taught.
And the last time you did
Play some ball with your kid,
You were closer to God than you thought.

Shiloah

Isaiah 8:6-8

We live "Las Vegas" lives.
Our attention is caught by the big,
the brassy, the spectacular.
The splashy events of life dominate the media.
We assume the big events of life are the important ones.
So when we come to the Bible
we tend to focus our attention
on the highly dramatic passages.

Isaiah spoke about people
whose attention was so completely riveted
upon raging rivers that they missed
the significance of a quiet pool.
By the pool Shiloah he found great personal meaning.
He spoke of the God he had encountered
in quietness, on ordinary days,
in the midst of the commonplace.

People involved in unusual capers
Get their names in the daily papers,
As do people who do unusual things—
Movie stars, congressfolk, shortstops, and kings.
Tales of the great and the weird have narration,
Especially those that may cause titillation.
Whichever the views I choose to peruse,
The unusual usually rules in the news.

And I scan the papers
     But seldom see
Anyone there
     Who resembles me.

People who've made a particular hit
Tend to be featured in Holy Writ.
Scripture is filled with unusual tales.
People fight giants or orgy with Baals,
Water is walked on, bushes keep burning—
This is the stuff of my Sunday school learning.
And my usual thought is that usually I'm liable
To find the unusual there in my Bible.

And I search the Bible
    But seldom see
Anyone there
    Who resembles me.

Isaiah spoke of a quiet pool
Whose waters sparkled clear and cool.
He paused for a drink at this spring serene
As a usual part of his daily routine.
Shiloah, he called this pleasant spring
And there he learned an important thing:
"Here," said he, "I find God's grace
Can permeate the commonplace."

We tend to comb life's grand events
for signs of God's omnipotence.
And so we feature the unus-
ual in Bibles and in news.
But meanwhile God's Shiloah hand
Is touching things we understand.
When meeting God, I note God hath
Approached me on the beaten path.

And I search the Bible
    And now I see
People there
    Who resemble me!

John the Baptist

Johm 3:25-30

Jerusalem's most highly famed,
And the aptest,
Preacher was quite fitly named
John the Baptist.

He urged repentance long and loud
(And made some cry).
That kind of preaching draws a crowd.
I don't know why.

His charismatic pleading way
Knew no rival.
Before long he was leading a
Great revival.

People came from far and near—
The strong, the weak.
'Twas quite a privilege to hear
This prophet speak.

His fame throughout the countryside
Gave John a lift.
Clerics often find that pride
Goes with their gift.

Preachers find it rather nice,
As you may note,
Being asked for their advice
Or for a quote.

When one has found his thoughts and views
Have great appeal,
Then starts to notice empty pews,
How does she feel?

John realized his own career
Had passed its peak.
For now the crowds were off to hear
His cousin speak.

John watched the dwindling attendance
And shook his head.
Of Jesus' rivaling ascendance
These words he said:

"He must INCREASE
I must DECREASE!"

That's not the way most preachers talk.
When in a jam
Does Oral Roberts send his flock
To Billy Graham?

John's ego has been verified.
Large was its place.
This man of pride still stepped aside
With humble grace.

Jesus spoke about John's worth.
We read later:
Of all the preachers on the earth
None was greater.

The Sons of the Prophets

Isaiah 7:3, 8:1-4

Some of us have had the chance
Of growing up inside a manse.
We got advice that then seemed ample
On how to set a good example.
We squirmed inside our Sunday suit
When dad related something cute
That we had thought or said or done,
To illustrate point number one.

We loved our folks, and they loved us,
So we didn't make a lot of fuss—
Although we wished they were less dense
When it came to common sense.
We wished they saw how we were squirmin'
When we heard mentioned in the sermon
Some little thing we say or do
That illustrates point number two.

Many a normal person did
Grow up as a preacher's kid.
And we can think of nothing that
Distinguished us from Mon. through Sat.
But Sunday seemed to be the day
Our private lives were on display.
For one could almost guarantee
We'd illustrate point number three.

The life we lived within the manse
Might have its minor irritants,
Yet most of us were happy creatures
While growing up with all those preachers.
Our lives were really rather mild
When compared to a prophet's child.
Those prophet kids faced quite a chore
And let this be point number four.

To illustrate, let us begin
With the names those prophets gave their kin.
Can you imagine how kids would razz
A chap named Maher-shal-al-hash-baz?
A boy would surely play the fool
Who bore that name through grammar school.
But Isaiah, man of fame,
Gave his child that frightful name.

He thought, "To keep God's message fresh
I'll wrap it up in human flesh.
Now when my boy comes in the room
Folk will hear God's word of doom.
Through him the Lord will have his say
'The spoil is speeding, hasten prey' "
And so his other son, we learn,
He called "A Remnant Shall Return."

Those days a prophet who was "in"
Wrapped his message up in skin.
Hosea's children also bore
Their father's thoughts on peace and war.
On prophet children we have dealt
Because I wonder how they felt.
I doubt they greeted with elation
Life as a sermon illustration.

When one is worried about doomin'
He hasn't time for being human.
I hope each prophet chose to live
With someone much more sensitive.
While they confronted storm and strife,
Perhaps an understanding wife
Renamed each little tad and tyke,
And called them Bill or Sue or Mike.

David and Goliath

1 Samuel 17:1-11, 38-50

I've noticed we tend to create quite a fuss
Over folks who seem bigger and better than us.
For the world is so vast! Its problems appall!
And our own minds and muscles seem puny and small.
So if someone of stature appears, who declares
He is perfectly willing to run our affairs;
And if we sense his presence is solid and large,
We are simply delighted to put him in charge.

Warfare's a prelude to power and wealth.
But for those in the ranks it is harmful to health
And no one, I guess, is especially thrilled
By the thought that tomorrow he might well be killed.
No wonder those Philistines rested their fate
In the hands of Goliath, who stood six foot eight
And weighed 265, whom none could subdue
In hand-to-hand combat! Of course!—wouldn't you?

Those Philistine warriors drew deep satisfaction
From watching Goliath just itching for action.
Ah, the bliss of the saint comes alike to the sinner
Who senses her money is backing a winner.
Out stepped that giant: "Come fight, he who dares!"
The soldiers of Saul knew the next move was theirs.
What an honor to silence that infidel's sneers!
But no one stepped forth; there were no volunteers.

Once-mighty King Saul was troubled and glum. It
Appeared he had no one to send to that summit.
"Some person out there in my timorous clan
Must be a faighter! Go find me that man!"
Off went his minions. (They weren't very sharp.)
They returned with a youth who played beautiful harp.
"Egad," quoth the king, "what an awful position!
I ask for a man, and I get a musician."

When you're dealt a weak hand the decision is tough.
Of course you can fold, but perhaps you could bluff.
Saul studied that shepherd. He looked mighty plucky.
In the right situation the boy could get lucky.
"I'll go with you, kid. You're my man in this scrimmage.
But of course we must tinker a bit with your image.
My helmet and armor should suitably hide
The scrawny, young teenager dwelling inside."

On went the armor. The results were très droll.
Young David appeared in his new warrior-role
Looking fearsome and macho—oh, you would approve.
But with all of that weight the poor kid couldn't move.
"I'm sorry, your highness, but as you can see
This claptrap is useless. It just isn't me.
Your instinct seemed sound, but I tell you, O King,
I am much better off with some stones and my sling."

Well, you know the rest. Goliath was slain.
It was David who cruised into victory lane.
And is there a moral? Well, one might be honed.
You see the results when Goliath got stoned.
But I think that this passage comes close to exposing
The folly of all of our post'ring and posing.
The tasks we are given will yield with less fuss
When we use the equipment that's suited to us.

Lord! Lord!

Matthew 7:21

Some Christians make me quite aware
Of their devotion, faith, and prayer.
While other people seem to lead
Their lives involved in human need.

I've noticed that I tend, quite oddly,
To find the latter much more godly.

Jesus in the Temple

Luke 2:41-51

We wait for what seems a bit more than eternity
For that magical moment of Pa and Ma-ternity.
Prenatal suspense seems to stretch into years.
It provides the occasion for worries and fears.
So when we see our offspring in wrinkled repose,
And it has the right numbers of fingers and toes,
From our hearts comes a prayer that is real, if informal,
"Thank God that our baby is healthy and normal."

Now normal is nice, but that term is too mild
To describe the uniqueness we see in our child.
For each set of parents knows perfectly well
That their own little tyke will achieve and excel;
And each word or action is carefully sifted
For signs that their darling is specially gifted.
Why, those children are ours! We know by all means
There is genius embedded down thar in them genes.

We've read the account in the paper, I guess,
'Bout the five-year-old boy playing masterful chess;
Or the girl who at six basks in critical praise
After flawlessly playing Chopin's Polonaise.
But we search high and low for some signal that our
Own budding genius is starting to flower.
But she's stuck in a classroom with some nincompoop
Who insists she can't handle the top reading group.

So it's easy to sense the parental elation
That Mary and Joseph felt on their vacation.
The big city tour was essentially done
When these parents lost track of their 12-year-old son.
I guess they were frantic, perhaps even wild,
As they tried to uncover some trace of their child.
They turned to the Temple for guidance and prayer,
And to their amazement young Jesus was there.

Where the scholars had gathered to pontificate
And engage one another in heady debate,
There in their midst sat this preadolescent
With a light in his eyes that was nigh incandescent.
His questions revealed a superb intellect
And were treated with deep academic respect.
That young couple perceived that, at last, they had run
Onto signs that they had a quite talented son.

I suppose that those parents, as other folks do,
Toyed with sending their boy to Jerusalem U.
It appeared he could easily garner permission
To matriculate soon with an early admission.
Their dreams of his future became crystal clear.
A quick Ph.D., then a brilliant career.
Or maybe he ought to try preaching awhile
For a good teenage guru is always in style.

When a child shows some genius, here are the results:
He is pushed into rigors more fit for adults.
And the pressure applied is the reason that plenty
Of prodigies burn out before they are twenty.
Thank God this temptation was duly resisted
By Mary and Joseph, who wisely insisted
That Jesus come home, as they certainly did,
And grow up in their house like a regular kid.

That's why, when at thirty, on that crucial day
That he started to preach, Christ had something to say.

The Man with One Talent

Matthew 25:14-30

Jesus, tell me why'd you choose
To fire such a cannonade
At that poor chap who wouldn't use
His talent cause he was afraid?
I think your point is very fitting
When many talents I command,
But not when I find myself sitting
With a single talent in my hand.
For I find your admonition to be fully involved and daring is a cinch to follow in areas where I feel competent and smart, but not in situations where I have one talent or less, say something vaguely connected with art. When I try to draw something I freeze up, my golden touch becomes dross. I can't even draw eight straight lines and come up with a presentable cross.
If ever I must draw a cross
I draw a blank instead.
I am completely at a loss
And want to hide my head.
At such times I can't be eager.
There is nothing satisfying
When my talent is so meager.
What's the use of even trying?
Jesus, you might show more grace
Toward people who don't try
Had you encountered face to face
A fearsome cross, as I.

But, of course, you did! Forgive me, Lord!
Well, back to the old drawing board!

Aarondipity

Exodus 17:8-13

Folk encounter fresh demands
When setting off for promised lands.
The freedom road for slave or serf
Soon leads across another's turf.
Established types don't want their daughters
Entertained by foreign squatters.
If you savor love and charity
Try not to be a refugee.

And so when Israel's freedom trek
Came near the lands of Amelek,
The angry, armed Amelekite
Forced the fleeing slaves to fight.
(It doesn't take a lot of brav'ry
To fight when you are facing slav'ry.)

Moses, as he was wont to do,
Bit off much more than he could chew.
"Upon this hill I'll stand," he said,
"Holding God's rod above my head
To show my men they fight this hour
Armed with godly strength and pow'r."

Now folk may conquer fearful odds
When they believe their cause is God's.
So Israel fought as if inspired
And prevailed—till Moses tired.
His worn-out muscles could not bear
The rod of God up in the air,
And as his arms began to droop
So did the spirits of his troop.
Their battle lines began to break
As they perceived the great Mose-ache.

Middle-aged prophets may be prone
To overtax their muscle tone;
They hate to think they've gotten older.
So two friends moved 'neath Moses' shoulder.
Aaron, right, and Hur on left
Gave his arms a mighty heft,
And bringing all their strength to bear
Raised Moses' arms high in the air.

Once more Moses on his height
Presented an inspiring sight.
His men knew God would have them free,
And fought to stunning victory.

Humanity oft gives its praise
To charismatic ones who raise
Their arms encouraging the rest
Of us to strive to do our best.

But let us praise a different sort:
The unsung ones who give support.
The one who cares and understands
And helps the great hold up his hands.
For history gives ample hints
That there's a "propper" behind each prince.

At the Altar

Matthew 5:23-24

This world should
Be a brotherhood;
On that we may agree.
And my heart melts
For everyone else,
But their hearts don't melt for me.

I never cease
To work for peace
In the human family.
So I get along
With the weak and the strong,
But they don't get along with me.

I love every man
As much as I can
To fulfill Christ's clear command.
But the folk that I see
Who refuse to love me
Are the people I can't stand.

Before the altar
I often falter.
I can't go through the motion.
I have the desire
But my sister's ire
Is spoiling my devotion.

Hasn't she heard
Jesus' clear word
That she's on the road to hell?
Her arrogant role
Is destroying her soul
And my peace of mind as well.

This world's a mess,
I must confess,
And it won't be any good
Till God gets my brother,
In some way or other,
To treat me the way that he should.

If you wish to increase
The amount of peace,
Here's a place for you to start:
Put lots of love,
Dear God above,
In the other person's heart.

Eutychus

Acts 20:9-12

Now I suppose that it is fair to speak of worship as divine
As long as one takes special care to omit the matter of pew design.
There is absolutely nothing divine about sitting in your average church pew—
Be it old or be it new.
Every pew has one board that cuts off the circulation just behind the knees and another board cutting into the small of the back.
That results in a coefficient of comfort roughly equivalent to an hour spent on the rack.
Another of the pew's dubious charms:
There is no place to put your arms.
In fancy churches with foam rubber cushions, be they Liberal or Othodoxix,
You will find an upholstery button caressing your coccyx.
Church pews
Are not good news!

When pew designers sit down at their drawing boards, they do not ask, "Will the congregation like us?"
No, they are obsessed with the challenge posed by the descendants of Eutychus.
Eutychus was the young man from Troas mentioned in Acts 20:9-12,
(if you care to get your Bible off the shelve)
Who was sitting in an open window, trying to follow the theological meanderings of the Apostle Paul
When he dropped off, both to sleep and from the ledge, undergoing a three-story fall.
And when everybody rushed downstairs to see if he was soffering,
He asked, in his dazed condition, "Oh, did I miss the offering?"

Well, you can see why church leaders, whether they
  are people of poverty or wealth,
Have concluded that sleeping in church may be hazardous
  to your health.
So pew makers have been ordered to build into their
  creations as much discomfort as the average person
  can take,
In hopes that the faithful will stay awake.
But if congregational somnolence is what they wish
  to abort,
I say, teach the preachers to keep it short.

There Is a Lad Here . . .

John 6:1-14

I wish I were a hero,
A martyr or a saint,
But so far I'm batting zero
For my life is rather quaint.

I could rage and shout like Amos
Or missionate like Paul,
But the chance of being famous
Hasn't come my way at all.

For the villains who need chiding
Don't live near my address—
Nor do kings who seek confiding,
Nor apostles in distress.

So I'm really getting nervous
That, ahead of me, there ain't
No act of thrilling service
That will make of me a saint.

No, the earth will not be shaken
By an act of mine—not nary.
For unless I am mistaken
I am rather ordinary.

I've come of late to ponder
On something I have read
About that day of wonder
When five thousand souls were fed.

It seems there was a lad
Among that hungry bunch
Who acted rather mad
When he offered Christ his lunch.

I bet others thought him daft.
I wonder what they said.
I suspect they grinned and laughed
When he gave his fish and bread.

"Five loaves . . . two fish . . . five thousand folk?
Now that is really dumb!
Will someone tell that crazy bloke
We'll only get a crumb?"

He may have yearned, as I,
To pull off some great big deal,
Move the earth or change the sky
Or produce a catered meal.

In that desert dry and hilly,
The simple country lad,
Feeling sorta silly,
Offered Jesus what he had.

But what he had was plenty.
Jesus took his fish and bread;
With it not ten or twenty,
But five thousand folk were fed.

From this I've come to understand
What cannot be denied:
A little gift in Jesus' hand
Is vastly multiplied.

Oh, I'll lead no great invasion
Of that I have a hunch;
But there may be an occasion
When I can share my lunch.

'Tis time for me to cease to rant
About the race I never ran,
And all I want to do but can't,
And do the things I can.

'Twould be nice to be a saint
All fleshly bondage fleeing;
Yet, I have no real complaint,
'Cause God loves this human being.

The Bible

The Sunday school where I was taught
Informed my friends and me we ought
To be completely overawed
When coming near the Word of God.

We learned good Christian folk were liable
To venerate the Holy Bible.
Our teachers flew into a rage
If dirty hand smudged Holy Page.
And so our fearful fingers shook
When we approached the Holy Book.

We all believed the Rock of Ages
Had placed his Words upon those pages,
And felt that God might strike us dead
If we made fun of what he said.
And so we read the Bible plots
As lots and lots of sober thoughts.
The humorous could never fit
My childhood view of Holy Writ.

But now, not wishing to seem rude,
I must deplore that attitude,
And raise my voice a bit to say
That I have found a better way.

I've found of late that I will tend
To view the Bible as my friend—
An older friend, still in his prime,
Whose thoughts have stood the test of time.

A friend who'll preach and plead and prod
To lead me in the will of God,
And yet like any counselor
Has small talk in his repertoire.

As any friend he will relate
Minutiae that is out of date—
And does not seem to mind the gaffe
That brings a chuckle or a laugh.

I find that I have really found
A friend when I can kid around.
That book upon my Bible shelf
Joins me in laughing at myself.

So I have found a friendly sage,
On each and every Bible page,
At whom I marvel—whom I doubt.
I laugh with him, and cry, and shout
of all the things I find absurd!
And that's the way I hear God's Word.

Christmas Eve

Luke 2:1-14

We place the precious Christmas manger
Upon the mantle, out of danger.
Hand-painted kings from Hummel lands
Are putty in young, chubby hands;
And glass-blown sheep are too exquisite
And fragile for a child to visit.
So, while we like them very much,
We ask the kids to look—DON'T TOUCH!

But once, I saw on a low table
Mary, Joseph, star, and stable,
The Babe, some sheep, and several kings—
Heavy, sturdy, rough-hewn things.
Here children dawdled, took their ease,
Read the sign: "Come, touch us, please."
And every child produced a fresh
Arrangement of that Christmas creche.

While donkeys watched the Baby sleep,
Angels petted woolly sheep.
And Mary rested from the noise
As Joseph chatted with the boys.
Each child knew to some degree
Just how that scene was meant to be.
I watched, with quite a little mirth,
Them orchestrate the Holy Birth.

So God, for her who understands,
Entrusts the coming to our hands.
God urges us now to begin
To place ourselves, our kith and kin,
And choose, among the many choices,
Where best we'll hear those angels' voices.
And join that Hallelujah Chorus
Knowing God's at hand—and for us.

So, friends, with bright and shiny faces,
The King is coming! Take your places!

Zacchaeus

Luke 19:1-10

On the brow of a hill
Near the edge of a wood,
Was the place where the house
Of Zacchaeus stood.
Such a house! Why it looked
Really more like a mansion.
The yard was enormous—
With room for expansion.
With the large swimming pool
And a neat tennis court,
Why, you'd think you were at
A vacation resort.
Now if you saw that house,
I suspect that you might
Think the owner was rich.
And by golly, you're right!
And you might think as well
That he'd have quite a long
List of friends come to visit
Him. Nope! There you're wrong!

For one thing 'bout Zacchaeus
Just wasn't too pretty.
He collected the taxes
In Jericho City.
That's how he got rich—
Not from his honest labors,
But by fleecing his friends
And then cheating his neighbors.
Those people agreed that
It just wasn't funny.
"He's built that big mansion
Of his with our money.
So if he acts that way,
We won't even pretend
That we like him at all
Or that he is our friend!"

Zacchaeus was wealthy.
He lived well, and only
One thing was amiss.
He was awfully lonely.
For when he came to town
And nodded, "Good Day"
The people around him
Would just turn away.
They showed him their backs
And averted their eyes.
And when he walked on
They made fun of his size.
For Zacchaeus was shorter
Than most other folks,
And shorties are often
The target for jokes.
So often he heard
A quite terrible tease
"Just look at that man
Walking 'round on his knees!"
His ears would get red
As he heard people snicker.
But he wouldn't look back;
He'd just walk by much quicker.
And he'd think to himself,
"Let them chuckle and roar.
I'll have the last laugh,
I'll cheat them some more!"

So you can imagine
The fuss people made
That day when Zacchaeus
Came to the parade.
Well, it wasn't one, really,
But it looked like it was.
People crowded the sidewalks
And watched hard, because
They all wanted to see
A great man of renown
Named Jesus of Nazareth
Come into town.

They hoped he would teach
Them some things about God.
But when they saw Zacchaeus
They said, "Now, that's odd.
Why would a cheater
So riddled with sin
Want to see Jesus?
We won't let him in!"

They stood on tiptoes
And made themselves tall,
So poor little Zacchaeus
Couldn't get close at all.
Zacchaeus tried hard,
But he just couldn't see.
So you know what he did?
He climbed up in a tree!

You must give him credit.
He surely was spunky.
But his neighbors just snickered,
"Hey, look at the monkey!"
They laughed till they hurt
And some started to cry.
At that very moment
Why, Jesus rode by.
He stopped by that tree
On the outskirts of town
And called in a loud voice,
"Zacchaeus, come down.
I'm tired and I'm hungry
And I just had a hunch
That over at your place
You serve a fine lunch."

Well, Zacchaeus hopped down
And he puffed out his chest.
He was proud to have Jesus
As his luncheon guest.
But the people around him
All started to fret.
You could tell at a glance
They were mighty upset.

"Say, we wanted Jesus
To come to our house,
But now he is planning
To eat with that louse!
Zach serves a fine meal.
He's a very good cook,
But, heavens to Betsy,
That man is a crook!
We just don't believe Jesus,
Who's pious and prim,
Should be messing around
With a person like him!"

But Jesus said, "Posh!
It won't matter whether
People approve. Let's
Go have lunch together."

After they ate, Jesus said,
"Zach, I've found
That you're not the most popular
Person around.
You're selfish and mean
And you cheat people, too.
Why do you suppose
That you act as you do?"

"I'd like to be nicer"
Said Zach, "if I could,
But I have to admit
I am really no good.
People don't like me much
When I meet 'em or greet 'em.
Since they won't be my friends
Then I might as well cheat 'em."

"That's nonsense, Zacchaeus,"
Said Jesus, "It's bunk!
When God makes a person
God doesn't make junk!
There's a wonderful man
Inside you," said the Savior,
"But you won't let him out
With your dreadful behavior.
Now you could become
That great little guy
Today! If you wanted
To give it a try."

Zacchaeus thought hard.
You could see him decide.
Then he leaped from his chair
And he hurried outside.
There were his neighbors—
The whole angry bunch—
Waiting for Jesus
To finish his lunch.

"Friends," said Zacchaeus
"I've gotten quite rich
By cheating you all.
But now I'm going to switch!
I've been wrong, and I see
I've been very mistaken.
So I'm giving you back
Four times what I have taken.

I'm going to be different.
And just to make sure,
I'll give half of my money
Away to the poor.
And from now on I'm acting
The way that I should."
Then he started to smile
'Cause he felt pretty good.

He remarked, "Thank you, Jesus,
For helping me see
There's a very good person
That really is me."

Well, of course, those folks wondered,
Just like people do,
If all Zach had promised
Would really come true.
But it did! And soon no one
Would ever deny
That Zacchaeus had turned out
To be a nice guy.

And we really should add,
Before this story ends,
That soon old Zacchaeus
Had plenty of friends.
They said, "It is funny
But we think, somehow,
Zach has started to grow;
He seems much bigger now."

But he was still short
Like he'd been at the start.
What those people saw now
Was the size of his heart!

Miracles

Matthew 14:22-32

I well recall my Bible class.
We read how Jesus trod the sea.
I often watched the little lass
Who sat two seats away from me.

I noticed she began to draw
In her book, among her notes,
A quite amazing replica
Of Jesus standing on two boats.

I thought, "A soul could not obtain
A statement much more lyrical.
That drawing makes completely plain
Her thoughts about that miracle."

And when we got to talking
She was clear about her views:
If a man goes water walking
He must wear enormous shoes.

She had chosen the empirical
As her daily regimen,
So she asked of every miracle,
"Did that really happen then?"

We haven't met in years.
I wonder what she'd say.
Do you think she still adheres
To that point of view today?

'Cause I have a new suggestion,
Which I'm ready to avow,
Of a more important question:
"Does that ever happen now?"

Not long ago I very nearly
Forfeited my poise and balance,
By taking on a task that clearly
Overstretched my meager talents.

I was going well, pursuing
Goals with vigor, vim, and verve.
Till I thought, *What am I doing?*
And began to lose my nerve.

Thoughts of failure and of dread
Were the ones that I could think.
I was in above my head
And I felt my spirits sink.

I was ready to give in,
(Which is something I despise)
Till a friend began to grin
As I looked into his eyes.

The message there was plain.
I could see that it was true:
"Stop acting so inane,
For I still believe in you."

That gave me such a lift!
I'm so grateful to that man!
For I made a major shift
From "I Cannot" to "I Can."

I finished simply great.
Oh, success was never sweeter.
And soon I could relate
My experience with Peter.

The way that Jesus reached to save
Floundering Peter in that sea,
And kept his head above the wave,
Was what my friend had done for me.

I was joyful and elated,
More than just a trifle awed.
Had I just participated
In a miracle of God?

I still have not decided
What took place in Peter's boat.
But I know the Lord provided
Strength to keep my head afloat.

I think that I could show
My friend, if we should ever meet,
That to traipse on H_2O
You don't need gigantic feet.

Has living also taught her
(I have a hunch it may)
That walking on the water
Is quite commonplace today?

Paul and Barnabas

Acts 15:36-41

Human beings should act moral!
With that we do not choose to quarrel.
Yet most of us have had a session
With what we termed an indiscretion;
And found, sometimes to our chagrin,
We quite enjoyed our touch of sin.

We do not choose, nor would we dare,
To make of sin our daily fare.
And while, at times, we've smiled or quipped
On learning that our neighbor slipped,
We tend to be quite tolerant.
For we have learned that humans can't
Be perfect in the task of living,
So it is best to be forgiving.

While most of us walk more or less
Along the paths of righteousness,
A few folk simply won't pollute
Their systems with forbidden fruit.
They look like us, but seem to feel
A special sort of moral zeal,
And find an almost strange delight
In knowing they are doing right.
They live their lives without a flaw,
Keeping the letter of the law.
And one might think that they, perhaps,
Have never had a moral lapse.
With folk like this, for heaven's sake,
Don't even make a small mistake;
For you will find to your regret
They can't forgive and won't forget.

When Paul was Saul we know that he
Was trained to be a Pharisee.
He learned in pharisaic fashion
To love the law with fiery passion,
And felt a mission to imprison
Those with different views from his'n.

When Paul came to his colossal
Appointment as Christ's chief apostle,
His former life was rearranged.
In many ways the man was changed.
But naught on that Damascus road
Affected Paul's high moral code.
While he, in theory, might embrace
That we are justified by grace,
His youthful legalistic ways
Were more than just a passing phase.

Paul felt that Christians should approach
Behavior that's above reproach.
His moral views were quite demanding!
He hadn't lots of understanding
For those who slipped—though he might try.
Paul was a quite judgmental guy.

So that's the context of the fuss
That came 'twixt Paul and Barnabas,
When they were starting to equip
Their second missionary trip.

Barney wanted Mark to go.
But Paul replied an angry, "No!"
He pointed out with frosty frown
How Mark had let the mission down
When he abandoned his fair share
And disappeared to . . . God knows where.

"I'll not attempt," the apostle glowered,
"Another journey with that coward!"

Barnabas insisted, "Paul,
That bright young man's received God's call.
I know last time he lost his nerve,
But now he really wants to serve.
Don't turn your back without a glance!
That boy deserves a second chance!"

When Paul took stands, we do not find
He very often changed his mind.
And he was sure it wasn't right
To trust that tarnished neophyte.
In this Paul stood quite resolute!
(Forgiveness wasn't his strong suit.)

This quarrel raised a dreadful wall
Between good Barnabas and Paul.
So much, in fact, they doubted whether
They ought to try to work together.

So Paul, at last, was quite insistent
That he would take a new assistant.
While Barney and his protégé
Could serve the Lord their own sweet way.

Paul was firm and quite unbending
And yet there was a happy ending.
As Barnabas believed he must,
The young Mark blossomed in his trust.
Mark brought the cause of Christ acclaim,
And wrote the book that bears his name.
His service had such great effect
He even garnered Paul's respect.

'Tis fitting that we all confess
The limits to our righteousness.
For, like Paul, you know we might
Be doing wrong, by being right.

The Temple Veil

Matthew 27:51

We've come to call God's Friday, "Good."
I'm not at all convinced we should.
It may be just a cover-up
To justify that bitter cup.

If *good* means we ignore the tragic
By using clever verbal magic,
And miss the sheer insanity
Of human inhumanity,
Then we should find a better name
To designate that day of shame.

Yet, one event that horrid day
Was very good in every way.
As Matthew tells the ancient tale,
It seems God tore the temple veil,
Which acted as a kind of proof
That God preferred to stay aloof.
And by this act of daring grace,
God left the sheltered holy place,
Taking on that painful yoke
To be involved with sinful folk.

In ages past, as you may note,
God dwelt apart and quite remote
Upon a high and holy place.
Man dared not look upon God's face.

When people sought the Lord's advice
Through ritual and sacrifice,
Why, nearly everybody tried
To act grown up and dignified.
God was straight, and rather stuffy,
And little "goofs" could make God huffy.

Now children bring some strange results
To overdignified adults.
One cannot choose to be aloof
When little ones live 'neath the roof.
All parents know a child soon teaches
The joys of playgrounds, zoos, and beaches,
How to laugh and have some fun.
And sure enough, before she's done,
A child weans her parental buddies
Far away from stuffy studies.

So it appears, the Holy One
Was quite affected by the Son,
Who coaxed God, as we might have known,
To leave God's lofty, heav'nly throne
And walk at eve in Galilee
Smelling the breeze from off the sea.
Jesus showed his Dad the worth
Of all the wonders of this earth.
They watched the sun rise in the east,
Enjoyed a happy wedding feast,
Helped a farmer sow his seed,
And shared concern for those in need.

God saw his world through Jesus' eyes
And dropped the lofty, royal guise.
God ripped the holy veil aside
To be with us—when Jesus died.

The Wisdom of Solomon

1 Kings 3:1-28

King David ruled with spear and bow
Yet sensed that blood had had its day.
He had in mind
His son could find
A better way.

King David, mighty man of war,
Now yearned for violence to cease.
So *Solomon*
He named his son.
(And that means "peace.")

King David planned most carefully
Before his son assumed the throne.
School for his pal
More general
Than was his own.

King David, commandant-in-chief,
Excused young Sol from R.O.T.C.
In peaceful mood
The boy pursued
An arts degree.

When Solomon at last was king,
He had no interest in the sword.
Another care
He raised in prayer
Before the Lord.

King Solomon asked God to bless
(As he took on that royal guise)
His mind, his head.
Here's what he said,
"Please make me wise!"

Now wisdom is a fitting quest
For anyone who serves or reigns.
  We do expect
  Folk we elect
Might have some brains.

War-weary subjects praised this king
Increasingly as time went on.
  He found the root
  Of each dispute
With brains, not brawn.

Two women each had birthed a babe,
But one child perished in the night.
  Each claimed as son
  The living one.
Now who was right?

The king was asked to judge this case.
He pondered, then addressed his staff:
  "The answer's clear.
  Use this sword here,
And give each half."

One woman smirked in victory,
The other blanched and pleaded: "Give
  The child to her
  For I prefer
That it should live."

And now a simpleton could tell
Which woman was the rightful mom.
  Oh, what a thing
  To have a king
With such aplomb!

So people praised the Lord by day
And thanked their God most every night.
  God had ordained
  A king to reign
Who was so bright.

So Solomon ruled forty years
In splendor, pomp, and opulence.
His style of court
We must report
Caused great expense.

He had a first-class temple built,
While sparing no expenditure,
And raised the dough,
As you may know,
Among the poor.

Those people rose in deep revolt
And overthrew that wise king's heir,
For he had spawned
A tax beyond
What they could bear.

So Solomon was bright, all right;
He ushered wisdom into fashion.
Yet now we find
His brilliant mind
Lacked compassion.

When Jesus taught his special friends,
He did not speak of having smarts.
He hoped that they
Would pray each day
For loving hearts.

Communion

1 Corinthians 11:23-26

This table now is simply spread
With little loaves of common bread,
Not pumpernickel, corn, or rye—
To spark the taste or please the eye.
Just bread—it's sold in any store.
I've had it many times before.

I am accustomed, when a guest,
To being rather more impressed.
I might expect a gracious host
To brown the bread and make some toast,
Or see his table was arrayed
With butter, jam, and marmalade.
Danish pastries filled with jam,
Some scrambled eggs with lots of ham.
This would impress me more. Instead,
The Lord shares common, daily bread.

I'll eat this bread, but I will find
Its taste won't linger in my mind.
This bread is easy to dismiss.
I've had ten thousand bites like this.
This bread, I think, in many ways
Reminds me of my common days.

Some days are vivid in design,
Resembling an exotic wine:
Days of joy and days of sorrow.
(One may well arrive tomorrow.)

But nearly all the days I've led
Are more like this plain, common bread—
Like, say, last 19th of September.
(A day I simply can't remember.)
It's gone, slipped from my memory.
Just as this bread is bound to be.

At this table I shall praise
The God who gives me common days.
And I shall live these days with pride,
Knowing God moves by my side.
For at this table God has said:
"I share with you this daily bread."
And by this Word we all are fed.

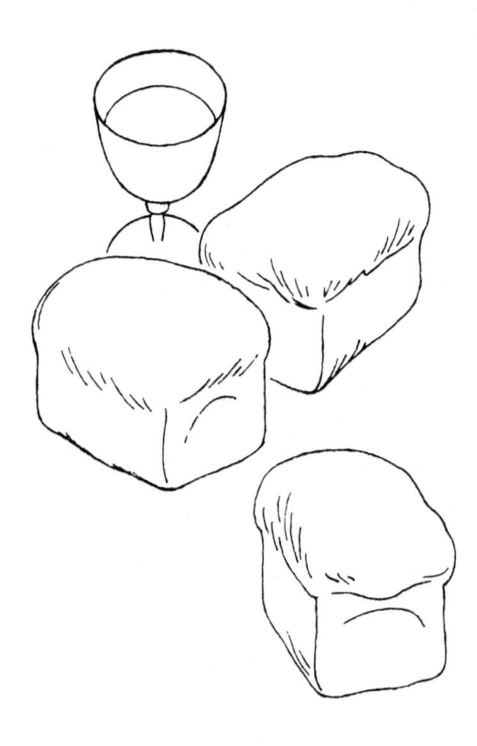

The Lucky Soldier

John 19:23-25

Honey, give your hair a comb;
Your soldier boy is fin'lly home.
Put on your brightest, finest gown,
Cause we are gonna paint the town.
Tonight we sing and dance and play,
For this has been my lucky day!

Shade your eyes against the glare
And look at what I'm gonna wear!
Here's the robe in which I'll dine.
Don't it look fine? And now it's mine!
Yes, mine! That's what you heard me say.
Today has been my lucky day!

You know it would have taken ages
To buy this on my paltry wages.
Such workmanship! It seems to gleam!
Just see if you can find the seam!
You can't? Of course, there isn't any.
This must have cost a pretty penny.

Now don't start any argument.
This didn't cost a blessed cent.
I got it from that strange buffoon
We crucified this afternoon.
His need for it was gone and done.
We threw the lots—and look who won!

God knows, I've taken many losses,
Gambling there among those crosses.
Perhaps my stars are rearranged.
I guess my luck has really changed.
This robe would go for three months' pay!
Today is sure my lucky day!

Fetch that calendar, dear mate,
And let me mark this lovely date.
Good Friday's what I'm gonna call it.
It won't matter if I scrawl it,
'Cause I'll remember, anyway,
What happened on my lucky day!

The Spies

Numbers 13:25-33

Opportunity, they say,
Approaches every door,
Knocks once before she goes away,
And then is seen no more.
Oh, I wish that I were wiser,
For seldom do I recognize her.

My eyes are rather weak,
And I simply can't be certain
That she's the one I seek
As I squint behind the curtain.
So, every time, the little lass is
Gone before I find my glasses.

Upon the edge of Palestine
Camped Moses and his band.
Those yonder fields, by God's design,
Would be their promised land.
They wondered in that desert quiet
Had they the strength to occupy it?

Moses chose twelve faithful men
To be his nation's spies.
"Infiltrate the border, then
Become our ears and eyes.
Report to us if you can see
The shape of Opportunity."

Forty days the spies were gone;
The time was far from short.
When they at last returned, at dawn,
They rendered this report:
"The soil is rich; the weather sunny.
It is a land of milk and honey."

"Yet this land we dearly prized,
We cannot take at all.
The people there are oversized,
And we are much too small.
They're giants—fearful, awesome thugs
Who'll squash us like so many bugs!"

But Caleb rather disagreed;
He was a different sort.
And so he raised his voice to plead
A minority report:
"We'll take this land without much fuss;
The people there are just like us."

He wasn't heard, of course
(Though his manner was defiant)
For no one will endorse
Going up against a giant.
To follow him might risk defeat;
The people knew when they were beat.

They later learned those spies
Had thrown a wicked curve.
Fear had clouded up their eyes
And destroyed their optic nerve.
But Israel acted on their fears,
Turned back, and wandered forty years.

I understand those spies
When I must make a decision.
With astigmatic eyes,
Can I be a saint with vision?
Oh, knocking Opportunity,
An ogre you appear to me!

Peter's Shadow

Acts 5:15

I noticed my shadow the other day;
And the child within who used to play
Kick-the-Can and Capture-the-Flag
Recalled the excitement of Shadow-Tag.

Shadow-Tag was my favorite!
"Step on your shadow—or you're it."
Such a scramble! I'll not forget
Maneuvering my silhouette.

Shadows, you know, are rather neat.
They stay connected to your feet,
Appearing docile—yet are known
To have ideas of their very own.

Many a time have I been tagged
When my body zigged and my shadow zagged.
How hard I worked to discipline
The antics of my prostrate twin.

Most children's games have one grand feature:
They serve us as a painless teacher.
That shadow gave me quite a sense
Of people and their influence.

I saw my shadow moving much
Beyond my range of reach and touch;
And thus I came to be aware
That though I'm here, I'm also there.

Of all the many stirring facts
Which Luke recorded in the Acts,
I've thought most often of the one
Brief scene of Peter in the sun.

You may recall the episode.
Peter walked along the road,
His thoughts much too preoccupied
To note the shadow by his side.

By that road, the sick had come
(At least the more adventuresome),
Simple folk who now were guessing
His shadow might bestow a blessing.

They reached toward him from couch and bed,
That his shade might touch the hand, the head,
Trusting that their convalescence
Might be speeded by his presence.

Maybe Peter never knew
About his shadow's rendezvous.
It's hard, of course, to realize
How we appear in others' eyes.

I'm sure he would have felt it tragic.
This trust in superstitious magic
Neither he nor God approved.
And yet, I bet, that he was moved!

To know your life has an effect,
That others view you with respect,
May agitate our human pride;
But, gosh, does it feel good inside!

There's much in life that we can fake
But not the shapes our shadows take.
We're summoned by the Holy One
To stand with Peter near the Son.

Matthias

Acts 1:21-26

What happened to Matthias
Is not especially clear.
What caused this very pious
Gentleman to disappear?

He is introduced in Acts
At a moment of success.
We'd like to have more facts,
But he had a lousy press.

He had supped at Jesus' table;
He had been the Master's friend.
He was the sort of able
Soul on whom we all depend.

We know he was respected,
Had a spirit kind and docile.
He was the very first elected
To the office of apostle.

He was honored by his peers
To receive a new vocation,
And he spent productive years
Doing church administration.

Yet after his election,
Scripture grants him ne'er a mention.
Should not one of such affection
Be devoted more attention?

What happened to Matthias?
I have an answer that
May reveal my inner bias:
He became a bureaucrat!

He had no exciting capers,
For there's nothing much to shout
About a man who shuffles papers
From the in box to the out.

We surely call the stabler
Folk to lead the church and yet,
The name of an enabler
Is quite easy to forget.

The Good Samaritan

Luke 10:25-37

A dad makes a fuss
When he goes on a trip.
He packs up his bags
At a very fast clip.
He checks out the plumbing,
The car, and the lawn,
And hopes nothing much
Will go wrong while he's gone.
He makes sure his wife
Knows the bills that need paying
And gives her the phone
Number where he'll be staying.
He calls in the children
At one time or other
To say, "I hope you
Will be good to your Mother!"
The children agree;
They smile and look pleasant,
For on his return
He may bring them a present.

Yes, when dads start to travel
They make quite a fuss,
At least in the families
That live around us.
And the fuss is the same,
If you wanted to measure,
When moms start to traveling
For business or pleasure.

With a dad leaving home,
Now our story begins.
He is saying good-bye
To his wife and the twins.
Each one gets a kiss
Then a hug or a squeeze.
As he walks out the door
His wife cautions, "Please

Be careful of robbers,
For I hear that they
Have been seen on the road
That you're taking today."
"Now, dear, don't you fret,"
He replies in a hurry.
"I'll be perfectly safe.
I don't want you to worry.
Take care of each other;
I'll miss you, but you'll
See me next week."
And he climbs on his mule.
With a wave he sets off
At a pretty fast clip,
Glad to be started
On his business trip.

Now this dad didn't show
That inside he felt funny,
For you see he was taking
A great deal of money.
And he had to admit
That his wife was quite right;
The road was not safe—
Especially at night.
But since he was going
To travel by day,
He didn't think trouble
Was coming his way.

All morning he traveled.
It seemed safe enough,
For no one he passed
Looked especially tough.
And as he was thinking
Of stopping for lunch,
All of a sudden
A rough looking bunch

Of robbers surrounded
Our traveling dad.
They slugged him and mugged him
And stole all he had.
They took all his money,
His luggage, and mule.
He lay by the road
And he thought, "I'm a fool!
I shouldn't have traveled
Alone. Why, I knew
Better. Now, just
What am I doing to do?
I'm in real trouble!"
And when he had spoken,
He noticed his ankle
Was twisted and broken.

He could just barely move;
And he started to hurt,
As he lay there alongside
The road in the dirt.
He lay there a couple
Of hours, at least,
When along that hot road
Came a fast walking priest.
"I'm saved," thought our hero,
"I'm rescued at last!"
But the priest didn't stop;
He went hurrying past.
"My good man, you've been
In a terrible crime.
I would like to assist you
But haven't the time;
And while I deplore
Leaving you in the lurch,
I must hurry on
To a meeting at church.
We're reading a number
Of very fine books
That tell what to do
For the victims of crooks.

"I'm already late;
It starts about noon.
I'm sure someone else
Will be coming by soon.
And I trust they will help
Straighten out your affairs.
So, farewell, my good man,
You will be in my prayers."

Off scurried the priest.
You could tell he was busy.
Our dad lay alone
And began to feel dizzy.
He hoped some kind person
Would soon happen by
'Cause there in that desert
A fellow could die.

Well, before long, another
Traveler showed
Up by the side
Of that hot desert road.
He stopped, and he looked
At our dad on the ground.
And he thought, "I suspect
There are robbers around;
And if I stop to give
This poor man some first aid,
Those bandits will get me
As well, I'm afraid."

So, he didn't stop either.
He simply called, "Peace!
When I get into town,
I will call the police.
I'm sure they'll send someone
To help you," he said.
"That's nice," thought our dad,
"But by then I'll be dead."

Time passed. It was nearly
The end of the day
When our dad saw another
Man coming his way.
"Oh no," he remarked,
"I can tell by his face
This man belongs to
The Samaritan race.
And all of my life
I've received this advice:
'Samaritan people
Are not very nice.'
They're dumb and they're meaner
Than most other folks.
And that's why we tell
Those Samaritan jokes.
I'm sure that the chances
Are awfully slim
That I will get any
Assistance from him."

He couldn't have been
Any wronger, of course.
That Samaritan fellow
Got down from his horse.
He pulled out his canteen
As quick as a wink,
Gave that thirsty father
A lovely cold drink.
Then cleaned off the blood,
All the grime and the dirt,
And splinted his ankle
So it wouldn't hurt,
Then carried our dad
To the nearest hotel
Where he could relax
And begin to get well.

So soon our dad lay
In a nice, comfy bed.
When he was tucked in,
The Samaritan said,
"Good luck to you, friend,
I must be on my way.
The doctor will come by
To see you today.
You've had a rough time,
But you're still pretty strong.
I'm sure you'll feel better
Before very long.
I know you were robbed,
So when I go, I will
Leave enough money
To pay up your bill."

And he did! Well, you know
It is really a shame,
But our dad never learned
That Samaritan's name.
And when he got well,
He remarked to his wife,
"I can't even thank him
For saving my life.
I'd send him a note
If I knew his address.
But I may never see him again,
So I guess
I can show I am grateful
By trying to labor
To treat everybody I meet
As my neighbor.
I hope this will teach me
To be a good friend."
And that brings this story
Of ours to the end.

Og's Bed

Deuteronomy 3:1-11

On many occasions we've raised a dispute
Re: the spiritual value of Num., Josh., and Deut.,
Sections of which we find truly absurd,
Esp. accounts of the folk who were massacred
In the conquest of this, that, or the other village,
The amount of the plunder, extent of the pillage.
These bloody statistics of each armed patrol
Are hardly the rations that nourish the soul.

Yet I have developed a strange fascination
With the tale of the war in the country of Bashan.
In the passage describing the death of King Og,
The author includes a unique epilog.
He describes in great detail the size of Og's bed.
It measured four cubits by nine, so it's said.
"His bed was six feet by thirteen and one half."
That is the gist of the king's epitaph.

What caused that old scribe to consider it vital
To pause in the midst of a bloody recital
Of the raped and the wounded, the maimed, and the dead,
With the story of Og and his wonderful bed?

I like to imagine the author was trying
To make the passage more bedifying.

The Other Nine

Luke 17:11-19

About that group of leprous men,
I get to thinking now and then.
Ten of them were in that band
Who felt the Master's healing hand.

Yet only one within their ranks
Returned to offer Christ his thanks.
While his response was mighty fine,
What happened to the other nine?

How could those folk have been so rude
And fail to show their gratitude?
In microcosm here we find
The thoughtless tale of humankind.

We live our lives at such a pace
We haven't time to ponder grace.
So I shall schedule in my days
Some time for thoughts of grateful praise.

But not today! I feel my oats,
I haven't time for thank-you notes.
So God who loves more than I ask
Is taking on a thankless task.

The Captured Ark

1 Samuel 4:1-11

I seldom get into a fight,
But when I do I know I'm right.
I feel the Lord of heaven would
Assist me if God understood
The issues and the atmosphere.
And so I pray to make them clear.

And that's the way the story goes
For human beings, I suppose.
At least, I see it very well
Within the book of Samuel.

The Hebrews had this reputation
Of being God's anointed nation.
They were chosen and consigned
To be a light for humankind.
Well, you can see how they assumed
This meant their enemies were doomed.
They'd count on God to intervene
'Gainst Canaanite or Philistine,
And felt they had a guarantee
That God would bring them victory.

So when the Hebrews fought this war
Of which we read in Samuel 4,
They knew the armies of those regions
Would melt before God's loyal legions.
But that day on the battleground
The Israelites were pushed around
By Philistines. Well, you can bet
Those godly folk were quite upset!

"What's happened to the Lord of Hosts,
Distracted? When we need God most?
We're getting licked! But now, we find
There're other matters on God's mind."

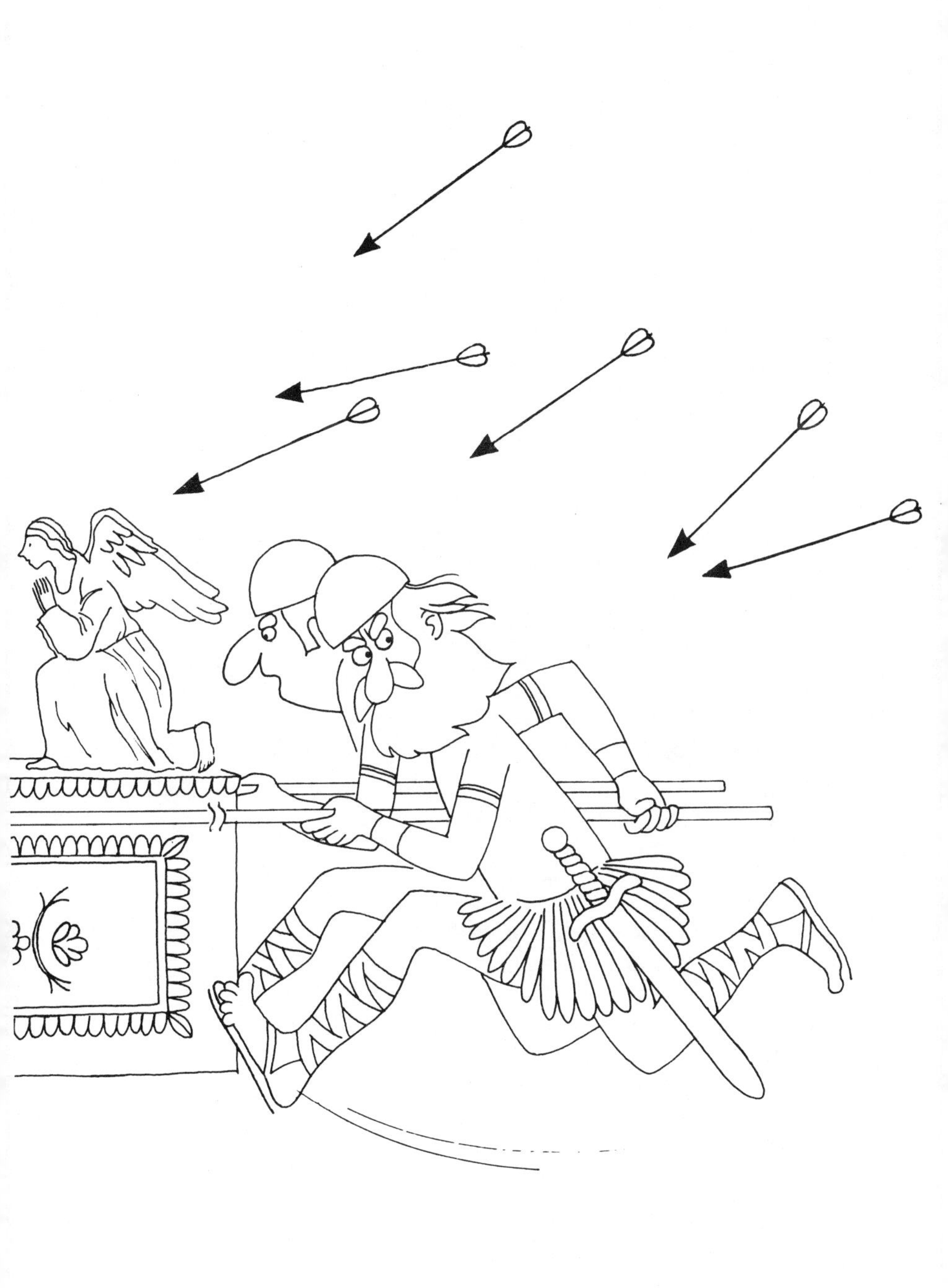

And so with the avowed intention
Of getting some Divine attention,
Those Hebrews pulled a clever stunt.
They brought the ark up to the front.

(Not Noah's ark, the one that's meant
Is the ark of the covenant—
That sacred chest whose very essence
Symbolized the Holy Presence.)

Now having brought that sacred shrine
Of God up to the battle line,
The Hebrews knew without a doubt
They'd put the enemy to rout.
(It helps an army's self-esteem
To know that God is on their team.)

But there beneath those desert skies
The people found a strange surprise.
That enemy refused to yield
An inch of barren battlefield;
And ere long on that fateful day,
The Hebrews fled in disarray.
And then to add a further woe,
The ark was captured by their foe.

Now surely every saint or sinner
Supposes God will back the winner.
So this is quite disturbing news:
That God would let those chosen lose.
And, I suppose, we really ought
To give this matter further thought.

For it appears, we all assume
In battlefield or locker room,
The Lord has made a sacred pledge
To give God's team the fighting edge.
And so we find most everywhere
That every fight begins with prayer.

But God, we learn, does not begin
To root for pious teams to win.
For those the Lord decides to choose
Will sometimes win—and sometimes lose.
So it appears that God is not
As thrilled with winning as we thought.

God may refuse to aid our strife
To teach us Yahweh's view of life:
The purpose of the human race
Is more than first or second place.

NO
YES

The Boy Who Said No

Matthew 21:28-31

The dad addressed Son Number One,
"There's so much work that must be done
To cultivate and till our land.
Today I need another hand."

"Father, had you any doubt
That I'd be glad to help you out?
I absolutely guarantee
This morning you can count on me!"

"How fine it is to know my brood
Is positive in attitude."
So mused the loving father who
Now approached Son Number Two.

"Good morning, Son, today I find
My work has gotten way behind.
I'm wondering if you would stay
Beside me in the fields today?"

The younger boy seemed unimpressed
And unmoved by his dad's request.
He set his jaw and shook his head.
"Don't count on me!" was all he said.

Our troubled father tried to hide
The turbulence he felt inside.
"Some day," he thought, "I'd like to know
Why that boy always answers no.

"We've had—myself and my good wife—
A positive approach to life.
Why, then, does our offspring give
The accent on the negative?"

Tears don't help when milk is spilt.
So bearing his parental guilt
(Which he kept pretty well concealed),
The father moved into the field.

The work had barely just begun
When who shows up? His second son!
The boy who just awhile ago
Had spoken that decisive no!

"Hi, Dad, can you still use my aid?
Let's just forget my brief tirade.
I'd planned to be with friends today,
But you need help much more than they."

All day amidst that growing crop
The son worked right beside his pop—
Who needed him because, you know,
His older brother didn't show.

His reasons? Well, we'll have to guess.
It does appear his easy yes
Did not commit himself to action.
So he fell prey to some distraction.

In this tale, Jesus bids us heed
The gap betwixt the word and deed,
Suggesting that commitment's essence
Is seldom easy acquiescence.

For oft a person really dares
To answer no because she cares,
And then we find when we begin
To do the job, she pitches in.

And folk who give a facile yes
Can leave a project in a mess,
For they're the type of volunteer
Who has been known to disappear.

So Jesus drew for our reaction
This picture of the saint in action.
His portraiture so clearly shows
The ayes are not above the noes.

Where Were the Men?

Matthew 27:55-56

Good Friday is surely a sordid affair.
The soloist asked me today, "Were you there?"
So I made a deliberate effort of will
To position myself by that Golgotha hill.
I felt so ill at ease; and since violence tends
To upset me, I looked 'round to find Jesus' friends.
I could see, as I stood by that gnarled gallows tree,
That the crowd was not large as I thought it might be.
And as I looked it over, it dawned on me then
That the women were present. But where were the men?

Where were the men? From my biblical classes,
I knew Jesus preached now and then to the masses;
But most of his ministry lived, ate, and spoke
With a rather small number of intimate folk.
And right off the bat they could see he intends
To develop a loving communion of friends.
They knew his compassion. You'd think they'd stampede
To find room near the cross with their friend in his need.
Their absence is puzzling. I ask it again:
Oh, the women were present, but where were the men?

John made an appearance, at least for awhile,
But the absence of others I can't reconcile
With the fact that they loved him. Why wouldn't you try
To be close to your friend on the day he must die?
I remember that night when he asked them to keep
Careful watch while he prayed. They had fallen asleep.
Do you think on that Friday when Jesus found harm
That his friends had neglected to set the alarm?
When the women reported the tears they had wept
Did the men say, "Oh, golly, we just overslept!"

Perhaps it is flippant to treat them this way.
The men could have been in a meeting all day,
Working like fury—with no coffee break!
Discussing appropriate action to take.
They may have condemned pagan Rome's persecution
And spread on the record a strong resolution.
Or maybe those men were just quite at a loss,
'Cause the women departed to go to that cross
Leaving the males to decide what they would.
But with no secretary, a man's not much good.

I suspect that those men simply were not prepared
For a rigged execution. I suspect they were scared!
And when they checked the action, they probably knew
There was nothing at all for a fellow to do
But stand helplessly by and allow Christ to die.
Now what's to be gained if they give that a try?
Look, a group of strong men, slim and trim, and athletic,
Wringing hands? Shedding tears? That would be so pathetic!
It may be to their credit; there's no reason to blame
Them for staying at home to avoid public shame.

The men were not there, if the theory is true,
'Cause they couldn't find anything helpful to do.
So how come the females were present that day?
Weren't the women as helpless and frightened as they?
Perhaps both were led by that social decree
That proclaims man must "act," but woman may "be."
Those women were helpless and weak, yet they dared
To be present with Jesus, to show Christ they cared.
His wounds gave them pain. How they flinched at each moan!
Yet their presence meant Jesus did not die alone!

That women may "be" while the menfolk must "do"
Is turning out these days to be far from true.
That a girl must grow up as a weak, helpless lass
Is quite soundly debunked in assertiveness class.
While women achieve and find new goals to seek,
I am wondering, Who will train men to be weak?
Can a man learn to weep, to admit that he's frail?
Will we ever consider this type first-class male?
Can the men stand today by the person who's died,
Or have we reached the point where we all have to hide?

There are times when I wonder just how much our souls
Have been warped by insistence on sexual roles.

The Fire Did It!

Exodus 32:1-24

When Moses had ideas for sharin',
He used to call on brother Aaron,
Whose voice had timbre, depth, and reach
(The kind that makes an awesome speech).
Oft Aaron spoke the anecdote
Or the bon mot that Moses wrote.
With pear-shaped tones he'd eulogize,
And people gasped and thought him wise.

The gift of gab can insulate
The public from one's mental weight.
Thus Aaron's golden eloquence
Disguised his lack of common sense.
To hear him speak you'd ne'er suspect
That he was shy of intellect.
So few knew he was ill-equipped
For leadership without his script.

Now few of us can really see
The foibles of our family.
We give our kin—both clod and lout—
The benefit of every doubt.
And so it seems quite obvious
That Moses acted just like us
In giving Aaron leadership
When he went on that business trip.

Only a fool would dare to toss
Aside a summons from the boss.
When Moses heard God's call on high,
He packed his bags for Sinai
And left his brother in command.
We may assume that Moses planned
That surely he and God could do
Their business in a day or two.

And for a time things went quite well
Among those folk of Israel.
Aaron's empty, vapid chatter
Didn't really seem to matter.
But then when Moses was delayed,
The group began to feel afraid.
"He should be back by now," they said,
"Something's wrong; he must be dead!"

The days went by; their panic grew.
Poor Aaron wondered what to do.
He didn't need a Gallup poll
To sense that he had lost control.
When leadership has been defective,
A circus often proves effective.
So he suggested to his staff
That they construct a golden calf.

The populace was duly told
To bring their rings of shiny gold,
And there amidst those desert sands
They watched the skillful, idol hands
Create a bovine deity
With agile spontaneity.
That work of awesome inspiration
Called for a pagan celebration.

They cheered and sang, broke into dance
And chug-a-lugged intoxicants.
They joined in rituals, coed.
(The details best are left unsaid.)
And at that moment, staid and stern,
Moses made his grand return.
Down the mount, across the gorge, he
Stamped into that frightful orgy.

A group that feels prophetic fury
Can sober up in quite a hurry.
No one cared to laugh or joke.
They hung their heads as Moses spoke.
"You folks will go down to your graves
With the mentality of slaves.
How can I get you all to see
That only God can set you free?"

Now leadership was far from bland
Whenever Moses took command.
He seized that calf and ground it up,
Mixed it with water in a cup,
And made them drink. "To what extent
Does this god give you nourishment?
Ask yourselves that crucial question
As you endure the indigestion!"

Not even Midas, we are told,
Enjoyed a meal that turned to gold,
And those folks felt a trifle crummy
With all that glitter in their tummy.
Indulgence wanes, repentance gains
When one is gripped by gastric pains.
So Moses ended the affair, 'n'
Then looked up his brother Aaron.

"Aaron, I can't understand
How you let things get out of hand.
I've worked with you—I thought you knew
What God and I have tried to do.
But when I leave for several days
You lead them back to pagan ways.
I can't see how you could begin
To get involved in such a sin!"

Aaron thinks, and then produces
One of history's great excuses:
"Those restless ones were growing bold,
And so I had them bring the gold.
We heated it, and in half
An hour there appeared this calf!
It was created by the flame.
You see, I'm not at all to blame!"

So Aaron says: In each event,
We're pawns of our environment.
We each walk with steady gait
The path determined by our fate.
So those who settle for his view
Are not at fault for what they do.
They simply follow their desire
And blame the product on the fire!

Christmas

Luke 2:1-14

We've moved! My, that's been quite a shock!
Now we're the new kids on the block.
We're still uncertain just which store
Contains the things we're looking for,
And wonder how the restaurants are
Or where to take our ailing car.
The unfamiliar casts a haze
Enveloping our nights and days.
Each morn some brand new task engages
Us with maps and yellow pages.

Our furniture seems out of place
Arranged in unaccustomed space.
We grope our way through life's affairs
And feel like those transplanted chairs.
For though our neighbors share advice
And really are extremely nice,
Life is not readily converted
For us, the highly introverted.
We sense 'twill take a little bit
Of time until we really fit.

We now approach The Holiday
With long-time friends so far away.
We trim these unfamiliar shelves
And feel so sorry for ourselves.
Till in our newish habitat
We turn once more to Luke and Matt.
Their words unfold a simple core
Of thoughts we've never had before.
That wondrous tale of stars and mangers
Is all about a group of *strangers!*

Looking from our point of view
We note that family was new
To crowded, busy Bethlehem;
And now we tend to feel for them.
We see how Mary labored with-
Out support from kin or kith
And in a manger laid Christ down
'Cause Joseph didn't know the town.
(He had no prior indication
That they might need a reservation.)

Yet God, the chief of all arrangers,
Blessed that young family of strangers.
Right in their midst God chose to dwell
And chose to be Emmanuel.
It seems in this that Heaven spoke
A special word to newish folk:
How oft we sense amazing grace is
Found in unfamiliar places!

We're trusting something rather pleasant
Will touch our lives this Christmas present!

Jesus Wept

John 11:35

Some folks can learn the Psalms with ease,
Can quote Shakespeare's soliloquies,
Can sing a whole Gregorian chant;
And some folks can't.

The "cans" oft use sarcastic banter
When e'er they run across a "can't-er."
"Don't claim your memory is hazy.
Tell the truth; you're simply lazy!"

But that, dear friends, is quite unfair.
There're conscientious folk out there
Who stuff their brains with dates and facts
And find them slipping through the cracks.

Take a person I once knew,
Her name was Kathy W.,
Who made a quite impassioned start
Toward learning Bible texts by heart.

Putting countless agonizing
Hours into memorizing,
Then realizing, sad but true,
A single verse was all she knew.

"The shortest verse in Holy Writ
Was written for my benefit."
Quoth Kathy, "I am not inept.
I've memorized it. (*Ahem.*) 'He wept.' "

To tell her that, in fact, the verse
Is "Jesus wept" would make it worse.
She gave it everything she had,
And one word out of two ain't bad.

Recycling

Habakkuk 2:20

Some basic rules define the source
Of pleasant social intercourse:
When friends share cookies (chip or date)
We don't return an empty plate
But send it back all nicely spread
With slices of zucchini bread.
And piques of proper social training
Remind us, as we're entertaining,
To see that we do not forget
The people owed a dinner debt.
So social bonds are smooth and flat
When glued with careful tit for tat.

But when it comes to heaven's grace,
Our tit for tat seems out of place.
How few of us command the wealth
To pay God back for kids or health,
For love, or comfort, friends, and talents—
Our ledger's wholly out of balance.
We can't pay back the Lord above
For all God's countless gifts of love.

God's love comes to us as a trust;
And when we understand, we must
Find someone else by dusk or dawn
Who needs that love and pass it on.

The Lord is in the temple; enter
Into God's recycling center.

Call to Worship

*Psalm 150**

Praise the Lord!

We never were intended, surely,
To come to church so doggoned early.
Yet here I am beneath this steeple
Gathered with God's dozin' people.
Just look at us! I might have guessed:
We all could use a lot more rest.
Perhaps this morn we'll be so blessed.

Praise God in God's sanctuary!
Praise God in the mighty firmament!

Good! He's going to read a psalm.
I love them, for they seem so calm.
I'll join the other people here
And let my mind slip out of gear.

Praise God for God's mighty deeds!
Praise God according to God's exceeding greatness!

The Smiths are late. They'll have to wait.
(My word, it's hard to concentrate!)

Praise God with trumpet sound!

I've come to find some peace and ease;
And so, Dear Lord, no trumpets, please!
Well I recall that dreadful noise
Committed by those Beazley boys
Who tooted here last Eastertide
And gave me thoughts of homicide.

Praise God with lute and harp!

Lutes and harps—that's much more wise!
And I'll lean back and close my eyes.

Praise God with timbrel and dance!

Do you suppose there's any chance
That someone will get up and dance?
Oh, no one here would be so crass!
Thank God, we're proper middle class!

Praise God with strings and pipe!
Praise God with sounding cymbals!

What?

Praise God with sounding cymbals! (CRASH!)

One more like that, for heaven's sake,
And we will all be wide awake.

Praise God with loud crashing cymbals! (CRASH! CRASH!)

Well, Lord, I guess to each one here
Your point is now completely clear.
You seem to feel your drowsy sheep
Can't worship well while half asleep.
We thought you were more tenderhearted.
But now we're up, so let's get started!

Let everything that breathes praise the Lord!
Praise the Lord!

*Author's paraphrase